a sk, half remembered

PARISHMITA BARUAH

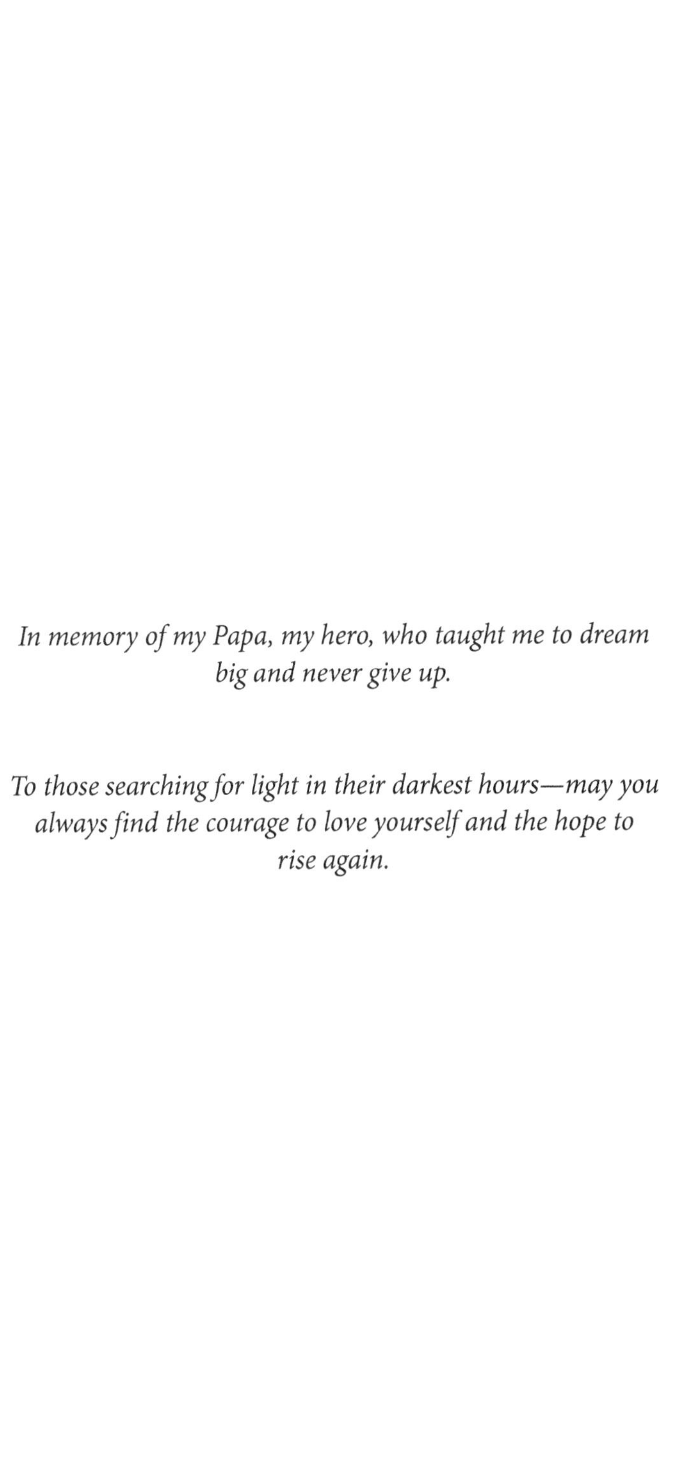

In memory of my Papa, my hero, who taught me to dream big and never give up.

To those searching for light in their darkest hours—may you always find the courage to love yourself and the hope to rise again.

"Don't tell me the moon is shining; show me the glint of
light on broken glass."

– Anton Chekhov

Contents

V – On Hope

VI – On Truth

VII – On Apology

VIII – On Poetry

IX – On Grief

X – On Self-Love

XI – On Things

XII – On Light

XIII – On Time

XIV – On Connection

Acknowledgement

First things first, a heartfelt thank you to my parents for being my eternal cheerleaders, even when I decided to scribble thoughts on scraps of paper instead of, well, doing anything remotely practical.

To my brother, Dhruv—thanks for always keeping life refreshingly unpredictable. Who needs peace and quiet when I've got you? To Namrata, for being the sister I never had. Thank you for always being so patient with me.

Aditya, you've been a perfectly brewed cup of coffee—warm, steady, and somehow making everything feel a little less chaotic. Thank you for being the quiet anchor in this wonderfully messy writing journey.

To everyone I've crossed paths with, whether briefly or for years—you've all left footprints on this journey. Some of you have been stars in my sky, and others... well, let's just say you've added dramatic flair to my story. Either way, you've shaped the person I am, and I owe a lot of this book to you.

And to you, my readers—thank you for choosing to flip these pages. Whether you're here for the prose, the poetry, or just stumbled in by accident, you're what makes this whole effort worthwhile. You give these words a home.

Here's to finding hope, light, and a little bit of love—both on these pages and in life.

A Note to My Readers

Dear Reader,

Thank you for picking up this little collection of thoughts, feelings, and the occasional overdramatic metaphor. It's an honor to have you here, flipping through these pages, and I hope you'll find a piece of yourself somewhere between the lines.

This book is a mosaic of emotions—some poured out in crisp prose, others tangled up in poetry, and a few that fall somewhere beautifully in between. It's about hope, self-love, heartbreak, healing, and all the little moments that make us human. It's messy, raw, sometimes even absurd—kind of like life itself.

To be honest, I didn't set out to write this book. These words were simply my way of making sense of the world— my anchor during storms, my celebration in moments of joy, and my companion in the quiet hours when the world felt too big and my heart too small. Somewhere along the way, they turned into a conversation I wanted to share. And here we are.

You might find pieces of your own story here, a heartbreak you've nursed, a triumph you've celebrated, or a hope you've held close. Or maybe you'll just find words that make you pause, breathe, and feel a little less alone. Either way, this book is as much yours as it is mine.

It's not perfect. You won't find neatly wrapped answers or life's secrets spelled out here. What you will find is honesty, the kind that comes with a few scars and a lot of heart. And maybe that's enough. Maybe that's what we need in a world that often demands we keep our messes hidden and our smiles flawless.

Some of you might breeze through the poetry, others might linger on the prose, and a few might reread a sentence just to soak in the words. However you choose to engage with this book, there's no right or wrong way to read it. Skip around, dog-ear pages, or underline lines that resonate. Let it be an experience that's uniquely yours.

Writing this book felt a lot like having a conversation with an old friend, a mix of laughter, tears, and the occasional "what even is life?" moment. And that's exactly what I hope it feels like for you, too. I want these pages to remind you of the beauty in imperfection, the strength in vulnerability, and the hope that somehow, some way, things will get better.

If there's one thing I'd like you to take away from this book, it's this: You're not alone. Whatever you're going through, your story matters. You matter. And even on the days when the world feels unbearably heavy, there's still light to be found. Sometimes it's in the kindness of a stranger, the hug of a friend, or the quiet strength within you. And sometimes, it's in a book like this, reminding you that someone, somewhere, gets it.

So go ahead, laugh, cry, sigh, or roll your eyes, I'll take it all as a compliment. And when you reach the last page, I hope you'll carry a little bit of this book with you, in your heart, your mind, or at least your Instagram captions/posts (no judgment).

Here's to hope, love, and all the messy, beautiful moments in between.

With love and light,
Yours truly

I

On Longing

The Watcher at the World's End

At the edge of the world, where the sky stretches endless, there lived a keeper of light. His days hummed quietly, as though he belonged to the machinery.

Morning, the fog rolled in, swallowing the horizon whole. He'd sit with his tea and listen to the gulls, though they never stayed long. They had wings to flee.

Evening, the tower would creak beneath his feet as he climbed the spiral stairs. He'd wind the machine, crank after crank, until the light flared.

Once, long ago, many storms back, she came. A stranger with windswept hair and laughter so unafraid, it startled the silence. She stayed two tides, maybe three, walking circles around him. "Why do you stay?" she had asked, fingers brushing the cold iron of the lantern.

"For them," he said, pointing to the dark horizon.

"Who will keep you?" she whispered, but the wind stole the words.

She was gone with the next moon, carried away in a boat too small. He still watched the light flare at night, wondering if it touched her sails somewhere far off.

Years later, they found the tower empty. But the light still turned—slow, steady, as though a ghost cranked the gears. And the sailors who passed spoke of a man whose silhouette still stood at the window, looking for someone who had already sailed too far away.

And maybe that's how it ends—his light, her sea. One calling, one leaving. Forever meeting at the edge of the world.

I want to find that old laugh again

I still see myself in that old jacket,
the one with frayed cuffs I refused to let go of.
I'd shrug it on, no matter the season, like armor.

I remember driving through the city at night,
the streetlights reflecting off the wet pavement,
and thinking, this is my world.
As if I could take it all with me.

I was always running late,
always a little behind,
like I was trying to catch up with time.

There was a day in early June when I sat by the river,
skipping stones, telling myself about my childhood,
how I wanted to be a pilot, soaring above it all.
My eyes would light up, then dim as I fell back into myself.

I remember the way I used to laugh- full, unguarded.
I wish I could take myself back to that,
to before the edges of the world started cutting into me.

I want to find that old laugh again,
not just smile to get through the day.
I want to be in those late summer nights,
when the air is thick with possibility,
and I'm not thinking about what could go wrong.

I want to see myself chasing after fireflies,
letting them slip through my fingers
without caring if they escape.

I remember the last time I sat in silence,
the weight of everything unspoken
hanging between me and the mirror.
I looked at myself, like I was searching
for a way out of my own mind.
I took my hand, felt the callouses
from all the work I've done,
trying to build something that would last.

I walked down to the corner
where the bakery used to be,
where I once stood in line for cinnamon rolls,
hot from the oven,
steam rising into the cold air.

I didn't say much.
Just stood there,
and watched the shadows grow long,
waiting for something, anything, to change.

II

On Silence

ПНАОИВ
РОСЕТЛА

A Table of Four

The silence sat between them, heavy as a stone, on a table of four, set for two. Plates grew cold; the candles burned lower. He reached for his glass, the scrape of it on the table sounding louder than it should, like the groan of a door closing. She didn't look up. Her hands were folded in her lap, fingers knotted tightly together, as if holding herself from falling apart.

It hadn't always been like this.

Once, they spoke in the soft language of coffee cups passed with murmurs, a hand brushing over the other's as if by accident. They found meaning in unfinished sentences and the pauses between words. Once, their silences were feathers, light and floating in the spaces where words weren't needed.

But tonight, the silence was something else. It wasn't the quiet of peace or understanding. It was the kind of silence that pressed into the chest, stole the breath, and filled the room with the things that could not—or would not—be said.

He glanced at her, at the way the light caught the strands of her hair. Once, he would have told her how the glow reminded him of fireflies in a jar. But now, the words turned to ash in his throat.

She shifted slightly, her chair creaking. Once, that sound might have been the start of a laugh—"This old chair, it's going to fall apart one of these days!"—and he would have promised to fix it but never gotten around to it, and she wouldn't have minded. But tonight, the sound only deepened the chasm.

Her eyes drifted to the window, to the moon that hung low in the sky. He wanted to ask what she was thinking, wanted to know if the weight of it all felt as crushing to her as it did to him. But the question stayed locked behind his teeth.

Across the table, her lips parted slightly, as if to speak, but then she closed them again. The silence pressed harder.

He remembered a time when she had told him that silence could be beautiful. "It's like music," she had said. "The pauses are just as important as the notes."

But this silence wasn't music. It wasn't even a pause. It was the absence of a song.

Finally, he pushed back his chair, the sound sharp and jarring. Her eyes flickered to his, startled, but she didn't say anything. He stood there for a moment, unsure of where to go, unsure of how to bridge the distance between them.

"I'm going to get some air," he said, his voice hoarse, foreign.

She nodded, her face unreadable.

At the door, he hesitated, one hand on the frame. He wanted to turn back, to tell her something but the words felt too small, too fragile to carry the weight of what needed to be said.

So he stepped outside, leaving the silence behind.

Inside, she sat alone, the room heavy with the presence of something lost. Her gaze fell to the empty space across the table where once there had been so much movement, so much light. She reached for her glass, her fingers brushing its edge, and for a moment, she imagined calling his name.

But the silence held her, too.

They stayed apart, bound together by the weight of a grief too heavy for either of them to carry alone.

A hollow place

I peel the silence from my tongue,
strip it bare until it bleeds raw truths,
until it's nothing but sinew and bone.

I hold it out to you,
an offering of all that lingers
in the void between us.

Will you cradle this heavy silence
in your hands, let it drip through your fingers
like sand slipping through the hourglass of our time?

I bury the silence in my chest,
deep where it festers,
where it becomes a part of me-
bone of my bone, flesh of my flesh.
It grows there,
roots winding around my ribs.

Will you dig it out?

Will you plunge your hands into the dark,
through the twisted veins of my buried past,
until you find the pulse of it?

Will you pull it free, hold it up to the light,
let it dry in the sun until
it crumbles to dust in your hands?

Will you take this dust,
taste the remnants of my soul, and find it bitter,
yet swallow it whole?

Will you look into the hollow place
where silence once lived
and find something worth keeping?

Can you touch what's left and come away unscathed,
or will my sorrow cling to you,
a second skin you cannot shed?

III

On Breaking

Still I Walk

I open my eyes, and the day is already too much. The street outside is busy with the tasks of morning—people rushing by with their faces turned down, their shoes tapping against the pavement.

A man in a red jacket lights a cigarette, the tip flaring briefly in the early light, smoke curling up. A woman with a shopping bag slung over her shoulder pauses to check her watch, her eyes darting between the passing cars.

A child's laugh echoes somewhere nearby, light and unburdened, but it is soon swallowed by the noise of engines, the hum of tires, the shuffle of tired feet. I watch an old man sit on a bench, his hands folded in his lap, as the morning paper lies unopened beside him.

A dog trots by, its leash dangling loosely, a slow wag of its tail brushing the air. Someone sneezes, someone coughs, someone sighs—every breath, every movement a small piece of the same story.

There's a vendor selling hot coffee. There's steam rising from the cups like mist. The world spins on, and I'm carried with it, but none of this feels real enough to hold.

Still, I walk, taking in the faces, the sounds, the small, unnoticed details, wondering where I fit into this endless loop. Each step a question I never quite ask. How can it be that I feel so lost in all of this?

It's not much, this intrusion

I've spent ages afraid
of the edge of my own skin.
time like a soft thread
between my fingers
is trying to weave
a pulse into me.

I long to rest.

I want a rest that cradles
the kind where you wake mid-dream
convinced you've been flying
only to find you've soared
into a stillness so foreign,
it feels like home.

Let me wander
into a life that spills less.
Let me sink
into something softer.
Let me tuck myself
into your pocket.

Let me slip into your shadow.

Be gentle when I arrive uninvited;

it's not much, this intrusion-
just the bell tower and a missing dove.

We'll stretch our moments into the space
between tonight and forever.
Every sunset will melt into honey and wild mint.

I'm not ashamed of my scars
but I won't speak
For the fire doesn't speak
of the burn it leaves behind.

All of this, I offer-
think about it,
with your roots and rust,
your eyes like bridges over rivers.

Think about me,
of my half-healed wounds and iron bones.

IV

On Renewal

The Garden That Grew Again

She used to say her marriage was a garden—built from seeds of promises, watered with time.

But in some gardens; weeds sneak in, roots twist unseen, and flowers turn to brittle husks no matter how hard you try to hold them. When her garden died, she stepped out into the world holding nothing but empty hands.

For a while, she wandered.

The world was loud when she'd been used to whispers. Empty spaces where he used to stand loomed larger than rooms, larger than houses. Some nights she lay in bed, the silence humming against her skin.

She wondered if the ache would always be this familiar.

But time has its own way of tending to broken things.

She found herself in an old market, where the air smelled of oranges and cupcakes. She bought a small pot of lavender, its leaves sturdy and alive.

It wasn't much, but it was hers.

She placed it on her windowsill. Every day, she watered it. The lavender grew. Its leaves brushed the glass, as if asking to be let out. Soon, she began collecting more—basil, mint, a yellow rose that curled toward the light.

She dug her fingers into the soil, felt life returning to her palms, her chest, her spine. One by one, the empty spaces in her home began to fill with green.

When spring came, so did her laughter. She danced barefoot in the little garden she had planted by herself. Her skirt trailed in the dirt. And when neighbors passed, they saw her glowing among the leaves and blooms.

It was then she realized something simple and true: not all gardens thrive. Some wither. Some die. But if you're brave enough to plant again, life will grow—different, maybe, but even more beautiful.

It does not carry your name

You've carried it long enough
the jagged stones of memory
piled high in your chest,
their weight grinding you down
to something smaller than you are.

It's time.
Set them by the river,
watch the current
strip their edges smooth,
take them where you cannot follow.

You are not the hurt that shaped you,
not the shadow carved by loss.
You are the light breaking over the hill,
the quiet unfurling of dawn.

Let the past sink into the soil.
Trust that the roots will take it,
turn it into something soft,
something green,
something bright.

You've held it too close
that heavy, rusted cage
of grief and blame.
It clings like smoke,
but you are not the fire
that burned you.

Set it down.
Let the weight unfurl from your hands,
let the earth hold what you cannot.
The ground has always known
how to cradle the broken.

You are not the scar.
You are the skin that grew over it,
the stubborn seam of healing,
the quiet strength that rises
when no one is looking.

Do not mistake the ache
for something sacred.
It is not your anchor.
It does not carry your name.

Walk forward,
one step, then another—

And when you walk away,
you will not feel empty.
Only lighter,
like a bird shaking free
of rain-soaked wings.

V

On Hope

The Boy Who Planted Stars

In a town where the night sky was swallowed by streetlights, the boy believed the stars had gone missing. He lived in a world of shadows and glowing halos, where no one bothered to look up.

He, too, stopped looking until one summer night when the power failed, and the world went quiet.

That was when he saw it: the sky alive with stars, scattered like silver seeds across a field of ink. He stood barefoot in the garden, the cool earth holding him steady. He wondered who had planted them.

The question followed him into the next day.

He took a trowel from the shed and began to dig small holes in the shadowed corners of his yard. Into each, he placed a pebble, a marble, a bead from his mother's old necklace— anything smooth and small enough to hold his little wish.

"Grow bright," he whispered to the earth. "Grow far."

His mother watched from the porch, a mug of tea cradled in her hands. "What are you doing, love?" she asked.

"Planting stars," he said without looking up, his hands dirt-streaked.

His answer made her smile, though she said nothing more. The other children weren't so kind. They laughed at him from across the fence, pointing at his empty garden.

"Nothing's going to grow!" they shouted, their voices shrill and sharp.

Still, the boy did not stop. Each evening, he returned to his little holes, tending to them as if they were the most delicate of gardens. He sat cross-legged in the dark, his head tilted back, his eyes scanning the sky as though waiting for something to echo down to him.

And then, one night, it happened.

A single firefly landed on his arm, its glow faint but steady. Then another came, hovering near his face. Soon, the yard was alive with them. The golden swarms, their light soft and trembling looked like stars set free on earth.

The children stopped laughing and pressed their faces to the fence, their eyes wide with wonder.

The boy sat still, letting the fireflies weave around him. The garden glowed, not with the stars he'd imagined, but with something just as miraculous.

He never told anyone, but he always knew: the fireflies had come because of the whispers. Because of the holes he dug and the hope he had pressed into the soil, as carefully as seeds.

The boy sat quietly, a small smile tucked into the curve of his mouth. He knew that sometimes, you plant things not to see them grow, but to believe they will.

Hope waits at your door

The morning breaks in quiet, steady light,
The smell of bacon curls up from the stove,
While eggs sizzle golden, on the pan,
The maple out front stretches to the sky,
Its branches spread like arms that hold the day.

Hope waits at your door, patient—
Invite it in for a cup of tea,
Let it rest, like an old friend,
Bake it a biscuit, warm from the oven.

Hope isn't loud or demanding;
It doesn't push or pull.
So, don't rush it, don't ask for answers,
Let hope linger in the quiet of now.

Then, when you're ready, rise and carry on,
Hope beside you, like sunlight on your skin.
It doesn't need to lead; it simply walks,
One step, then the next, and you will see.

VI

On Truth

The Girl Who Spilled Light

In this city, they speak in straight lines. Words are engineered like bridges. The air hums with precision. Yet it feels thin, as though it cannot carry the weight of anything tender.

She wanders, clutching the fragments of what they call excess—an ache, a sigh, the memory of rain slipping down her wrist.

They tell her to measure her days in tasks completed. And then to stack her hours like stones until she builds a tower high enough to forget what lies beneath. But at night, she lit small lamps and their wicks reminded her of stolen moments—laughing too loudly, crying too long, holding too tightly.

The lamps sputter against the wind, and she crouches close, guarding their flames.

Once, she found a room filled with others like her. Their eyes glinted and they spoke in whispers, trading the weight of our hearts. One told her of a garden where emotion blooms, its vines spilling over the edges.

Outside, the world burns clean, unfeeling, white-hot with logic. She watches the smoke rise, thick with the scent of things erased—letters, melody, and the warmth of a hand. They say this fire purifies. She knows it only hollows.

Still, she wanders. Still, she carries the lamps, though she does not know if they will outlast the wind. Perhaps they will not. But perhaps the flicker of their light is enough.

She wants to go out like a lamp shattered in the dark, spilling light where none should be.

I'd rather break

I don't regret
feeling everything the way I do—
so deeply, so fully,
like my heart is made of open doors,
always welcoming the world in.

I don't regret the tears that come easy,
that spill over at the sight of beauty,
or even at the weight of pain.
It is in those tears,
I've felt life in all its messy, tender forms.

I've been told
I'm too sensitive, too soft,
as if it's a weakness,
as if the ability to feel deeply
is a flaw that needs mending.

But I know it's not.
It's a gift—
to absorb the sunsets,
the feel the wind on my skin,
to bloom the way flowers do,
to feel the earth beneath my feet
and let it move me.

I carry it all,
every joy and ache,
every tender moment
tucked into my chest.
And yes, it hurts sometimes—
to love, to lose,
to care for the world so much
that it breaks you open.
But I don't regret a single crack.

I don't regret the way my heart stretches,
the way it holds everything inside—
the sadness, the wonder, the beauty of it all.

I don't regret feeling so much,
because in this world,
where so much is fleeting,
I've learned that to feel deeply
is to live fully.

And if that means I break sometimes,
if that means the tears come easily,
so be it.

I'd rather break
than be numb
to the beauty of this life.

VII

On Apology

The Anatomy of an Apology

It started one afternoon when the sky hung heavy with rain.

She had stood in the doorway, his coat in her hands, her fingers running across the fabric. The argument had been loud, something that never felt like it could be patched. But as he turned to leave, his back stiff, the silence between them felt like a wound no one had the words to stitch.

The words hadn't come for hours after. They hung in the air like smoke, difficult to breathe around. She had cleaned the kitchen, her hands moving mechanically over the dishes, trying to find a way to quiet the storm in her chest.

The words were there, but they didn't fit. They weren't enough. They never seemed enough. She stared at the screen of her phone, a knot tightening in her throat.

The next morning, he came to the door. His hand trembled when he reached for the knob, and when she opened the door, his voice cracked before he could say anything.

"I didn't mean it," he whispered. "I didn't mean any of it."

She had heard apologies before, so many times.

The way he stood there, shoulders hunched under the weight of it, was more than the words themselves. There was a tenderness to it, a rawness that made her heart ache. He wasn't asking for forgiveness, not yet.

He was just offering what was left of himself.

She wasn't sure if it was him she was speaking to or the memory of what they had become after all the hurt had settled in.

He stepped closer, hands empty, no longer holding onto the excuses they had been hiding behind. "I just need you to know I see it. I see how I hurt you."

And in that moment, the apology wasn't the words.

It was in the way he stepped back, giving her space, not demanding a response. It was in the way he held his breath as if he wasn't sure if she would close the door or open her arms. It was in the quiet between them, where the possibility of something different could bloom—if she let it.

She didn't answer right away, and maybe that was its own kind of apology. That in the silence, in the waiting, there was room to breathe again, to choose if healing could start.

But in the end, it wasn't about fixing everything all at once. It was simply about meeting each other in the mess of their mistakes, each willing to be seen, without pretense. Without guarantees.

"Stay," she finally said, the word barely a whisper.

He stepped inside, his coat still in her hands. And in the quiet of that moment, the apology settled between them. It was not perfect but real. The kind that could only exist if both people were willing to carry its weight, together.

The storm outside had passed, but the sky was still heavy.

An apology is a door

In the beginning, it is silence—
a shallow breath held too long in the ribs,
the weight of unsaid things sinking into the floorboards.

It lingers there, thick as smoke,
coiling through the cracks of a closed door.
No one dares touch it.

But then, it stirs—
a tremor in the voice,
a hesitating hand,
twitchy fingers.

Then it comes
and lands fragile in the room,
like a pup with broken limbs.

But the real apology
is the way they bow their head,
It is in the slow surrender of pride.

An apology is not words;
it is the needle that stitches
the torn cloth of time.

It is the offering
of one's own trembling hands,
palms turned upward, empty,
inviting trust to bloom again.

But sometimes,
the apology arrives too late,
after the flowers have withered,
after the soil has hardened to stone.
Even then, it tries,
placing seeds in the cracks,
whispering prayers to the rain.

An apology is a door
to a possibility, but
it carries no guarantees,
only the weight of its own honesty,
its willingness to kneel,
to bleed, to begin again.

And then,
if the heart it knocks upon
chooses to answer,
there blooms the faintest scent of second chances,
to show even broken things can breathe again.

VIII

On Poetry

The Weight of Words

There was a boy who never spoke. His words, when they came, were soft and hesitant in his mind. People couldn't hear them. But they noticed how his silence wrapped around him like a cloak, how his eyes flickered with thoughts he never shared.

He sat by the window of his small room, staring at the world outside. The sky stretched like a bruised canvas, swollen and waiting. That's when the notebook appeared.

It was a simple thing, paper worn at the edges, its pages hungry for something. The boy opened it and his pen hovered over the blank page. He had always watched others speak, their words filling the air, like they could grasp something real with each sentence.

Then a single word fell from his mind and into the paper. Then another. And another.

It wasn't long before the page was filled. The words came in uneven rhythms. His pen moved fast, driven by something he couldn't name.

It wasn't a story, just fragments; pieces of himself scattered across the page. He poured everything into it: the weight of the silence he carried, the way his chest felt too small for his thoughts, the way his heart beats louder than anything else.

When he finished, he sat back and stared at the page. It wasn't perfect. The lines didn't rhyme, the sentences didn't follow any rules. It was raw and messy, but it was his.

He had given his grief a shape, his pain a form. He had, for the first time, spoken—not with his voice, but with something deeper.

He walked outside; walked through the crowded streets. People still spoke their busy, empty words and he still carried his grief, but it no longer weighed him down in the same way. He had placed it somewhere, put it into words that no longer haunted him from within. The notebook, the ink, the act of creating—it had freed him, just a little.

He wrote more. He wrote of the rain, of the moonlight that washed over the city, of the things he had never said. And in those moments, he understood what poetry was.

It was a release, a bridge between the self and the world. It was the space where the unspoken could find a home, where grief could find its voice, where joy could be given the wings to soar.

Poetry had given him a language for all that he had carried, all that had once been too heavy to hold. But now, not as a burden, but as a part of who he was. The weight of the words, now, was his to bear.

Grief comes to whoever loves

I carry grief like a rock in my chest,
heavy and lodged in quiet places.
But I've learned to fold it into words—
to trace its edges with ink,
to lay it down in pages,
so I don't have to carry it in my bones,
so I can breathe without the weight of it pressing.

Each time I write, I throw it into the sky,
let it scatter like white dandelions in the wind,
and for a moment,
I am light,
as though I can stand on tiptoe,
unburdened by the endless ache
of holding the world inside me.

There is a strange comfort in knowing
that grief is not mine alone—
that the pain I carry is echoed
in hearts across time and space,
like a song sung by voices
I've never heard,
but somehow, I understand.

We are all walking the same road,
our feet heavy,
but our hands reaching
for the same thread of hope—
that the words we speak,
the words we write,
can hold us,
can keep us from falling apart,
can remind us
that we are not alone.

And when the weight becomes too much,
I remind myself that my pain
is not new,
that somewhere, someone else has lived through
the same story,
the same heartbreak,
the same ache in their bones.
And in that, I find a strange kind of peace,
for I know that grief,
comes to whoever loves.

IX

On Grief

Grief Shows Up in the Little Things

Grief shows up in the little things. In the half-drunk cup of coffee left on the kitchen counter, the one she brewed but couldn't bring herself to sip. It's in the hum of the refrigerator at 2 a.m., when the house is too quiet.

Grief sits in the laundry she keeps forgetting to fold, in the mismatched socks she can't bother to pair. It's in the dust gathering on the books she promised she'd read someday.

Grief rides with her in the car, in the way she turns the volume up when a certain song comes on. It's in the supermarket aisle, standing too long in front of the cereal boxes because she can't remember which one used to feel like home.

It hides in the chipped coffee mug, the one she keeps reaching for even though it leaks, because it feels wrong to throw it away. Grief clings to the sunlight filtering through the curtains, painting gold but without warmth.

It sits in the toast left untouched on the plate, in the way the butter knife rests awkwardly on the edge, like it doesn't belong. She stares at the calendar pinned to the fridge, dates that mean nothing now, and wonder if it's possible to feel emptier than a blank square.

In the evenings, she feels it most in the soft yellow glow of the lamp beside the couch. The TV drones on about nothing, filling the air with background noise.

She's staring at the glass of water on the coffee table, condensation pooling beneath it like the tears she won't let fall tonight. She tells herself to take a sip, but it's easier to just let it sit there, untouched, as if by leaving it, she can leave herself untouched too.

Grief sneaks into the mundane, the cracks between what she does and what she feels. It's in the shoes by the door, the ones no one wears anymore but she can't bring herself to move. Grief is the weight in her limbs when she tries to vacuum the rug, the way she sits down halfway through and forgets why she started.

But sometimes, she notices other things, too. The way the sunlight plays on the clean dishes, casting rainbows through water droplets. The way the kettle's whistle breaks the silence, a sound that sounds alive.

She feels the warmth of the blanket she curls up under, how it feels like a hug.

Grief lives in the mundane, but so does healing. It's in the rituals she repeats, even when they feel pointless. It's in the way she pours herself another cup of coffee.

And how she let herself be. She let herself be.

The softest, heaviest thing

Grief is cold.
It's the kind of chill that settles deep,
burrowing under your skin,
finding all the empty spaces inside you,
filling them with a certain ache.

It creeps in when the world falls silent,
when the night wraps itself around you,
and you pull the blanket tight,
trying to shut it out,
trying to find warmth,
but it finds a way in,
seeping through every crack,
every breath,
every thought.

There are days I want to curl up,
hide beneath the layers of fabric,
pretend the world is small,
and I can fit everything inside it—
but grief is bigger than that.

It stretches out,
slow and relentless,
like winter creeping over the earth,
turning everything it touches cold.

It whispers in the quiet,
when the house is still,
and the dark feels endless,
reminding you of everything
that has slipped through your fingers.

I've known the ache of missing,
the ache of wanting,
the ache of holding on to what's already gone.
And sometimes it feels like
I'm just gathering shards,
trying to piece together what once was whole,
even when I know
there are pieces that will never fit again.

Grief isn't loud,
it's the softest, heaviest thing—
a constant shadow,
a quiet companion.
It comes when you least expect it,
when you think you're fine,
and then suddenly,
there it is, cold as ever,
reminding you of every goodbye,
every heartbreak you've ever known.

X

On Self-Love

In the Smallest of Rebellions

Self-love hides in the clatter of dishes. In the way her hands move methodically, scrubbing away yesterday's crumbs. It's there, in the way she lets herself pause before the last dish, staring out of the kitchen window at a sky that doesn't demand anything of her.

It waits in the folds of fresh laundry. The way she sits cross-legged on the bed, and smooths out the wrinkles in her favorite T-shirt, the one she wears when she wants to feel like herself.

It lives in the ordinary.

In the act of buttering a toast, spreading it to every corner. It is in her sigh she lets out as she settles into her chair after a long day. It's in the cup of tea she makes with some ginger and honey. It's in the desire to let the steam rising to meet her face, a fleeting warmth she likes in the winter.

It's there in the decision to sweep the floor on a quiet evening, the brush catching dust and lost strands of hair.

And sometimes, self-love is nothing more than watering a plant.

The lazy tilt of the jug, the glint of water catching light as it spills onto soil. It's in the way she buys flowers for the table, arranging them clumsily in a jar.

Self-love is not in the grand gestures; it's in the unnoticed moments.

The way she closes her eyes when the afternoon sun streams through the blinds, soaking up the warmth as if storing it for darker days. It's the way she stretches her legs on the couch, unashamed of taking up space.

And on the days when it feels like too much, when the weight of everything pulls her down, self-love is the smallest of rebellions.

It's letting the phone ring unanswered. It's curling up with a book she has read a hundred times, or watching a movie that makes her smile.

Familiarity holds her like a lullaby and whispers to her,

"You're here. You're trying. You're enough."

Growing differently

It's been ages since I felt the earth between my fingers,
since I let the wind run its fingers through my hair
and tell me the things I once ignored.

Now, here, I grow differently.
Let my hair fall loose, unruly, like vines reaching for the
ground,
hiding the traces of paths I've left behind.
Let my hands be calloused with choices,
each line a road I didn't take,
each scar a truth I refused to bury.

Let the smoothness crack,
let it crumble like old paint on walls.
Let my shape shift,
not for someone else,
but for me.

Once, I bit my tongue until it bled,
but I learned the taste of iron and knew—
this mouth was meant to speak
and not to be held shut by someone else's story.

Let them look, let them wonder—
I'm no longer afraid of being too much.

I've spent years in silence,
And studied every corner of myself, even the ones I feared.
And now, I walk among the ruins I built,
and I am not ashamed of what remains.

XI

On Things

The Things in the House Have Stopped Waiting

In the small hours of the morning, before the house wakes, the kettle begins its quiet labor; steam rises like a ghost that wants to escape the mouth of it. The handle of the mug warms to the touch of hands and the table stands firm with all its scars and scratches.

When he left, he didn't take much. A few books, some clothes, and the photograph from the mantle. But the objects he left behind—they stayed, tethered to their purpose. As though his absence were a temporary thing.

The chair still leans slightly to one side, remembering the weight of his body.
The sink still wears our stains like badges.

Sometimes, she watches the curtains in the late afternoon light, the way they flutter against the open window. She thinks of him then, the way he used to fold the sheets. She never got it right when she tried to mimic him.

The things in the house have stopped waiting. The kettle whistles with a sharper note now. The floor creaks louder than it used to. Even the doorknob feels colder, as if bracing itself for hands that never come. But there is no bitterness in them, no accusation.

If she listens closely, she can almost hear their stories—how they gave, and gave, and gave, until all that was left was the echo of a life once lived between their edges.

The things around us

Look at the things around you.
Look at how the lamp stands in the darkness,
how the table waits, steady and still,
how shadows follow you across the floor
as if they know their place.

There is a sort of calmness in them.
In the way the books rest easy on their spines,
the keys linger, unworried,
in bowls by the door,
In the way curtains hold the evening
gently at bay.

In the way the rope bends and bends,
the faucet whispers
as it lets water slip away.

Only if we were as forgiving as them.
As a doorframe,
taking the weight
of every hand
that leans,
every shoulder
that presses
on its edge.

XII

On Light

The Old Man and Dog

The old man had nothing left but time. It stretched before him like the empty plains he once drove across, endless and barren. His house was quiet now, too big for just one man. The chairs at the table sat undisturbed, the bed untouched on one side. His world had grown smaller—just a recliner, a dusty lamp, and the sound of the wind outside.

He didn't want a dog.

But the neighbor's girl knocked on his door one morning, holding a trembling bundle of fur with eyes like molten gold. "He wandered into our yard," she said. "Dad says we can't keep him. He needs someone, and… maybe you do too."

He opened his mouth to refuse, to explain that he couldn't take care of anything anymore—not a dog, not himself. But the pup leaned forward, pressing its wet nose into the man's weathered palm, and something in his chest cracked open.

The dog stayed.

At first, they were strangers. The old man fed him, let him sleep by the fire, and called him "Dog" because he didn't have the heart to name him. But Dog was patient. He followed the man through the house, his paws clicking softly on the wood floors.

He sat by the recliner, his golden eyes watching every movement like the man was the only thing in the world worth seeing.

The mornings began to change. The old man would wake to the sound of paws padding across the room, followed by a soft whine. Dog had taken to sitting by the window, watching the sunrise like he understood its quiet beauty.

The old man found himself shuffling to the kitchen earlier than usual, brewing a pot of coffee and setting aside a corner of toast for Dog, who devoured it as crumbs clung to his nose.

One day, Dog pranced into his room, proudly carrying a sock. It was an old one, its mate long gone, but the dog held it like a prized possession. The old man chuckled and traded the sock for a rub behind the ears.

"You're a strange one," he said, his voice softer than it had been in years.

Dog barked—a sharp, joyful sound—and ran to the leash hanging by the coat rack. He wagged his tail so hard his whole body wiggled, and the man couldn't help but chuckle.

"Fine, you win," he muttered, clipping the leash on.

Outside, the air was crisp and alive. Dog bounded ahead, sniffing everything, tugging the man out of his careful, heavy steps. They walked farther than the old man had in years, past the quiet houses and into the park, where sunlight spilled through the trees.

Dog stopped at a patch of clover, turning to look at him with those golden eyes. The man knelt slowly, his knees creaking, and ran his fingers through the soft fur.

Later, back home, he opened a can of dog food with a kind of purpose, the metallic click of the lid echoing in the small kitchen. He swept up the clumps of fur that gathered in the corners, muttering under his breath about the mess but secretly grateful for the signs of life filling the space.

That night, he sat by the fire, Dog curled at his feet. He stroked the pup's ears and whispered,

"Guess I'll have to give you a name, huh?" Dog wagged his tail happily.

The days grew longer after that. The old man started to leave the house more with Dog trotting beside him. He began to laugh again, small bursts at Dog's antics—the way he chased leaves, or how he tried to bark at his own reflection.

He even began humming softly as he moved through the house, a habit he thought he'd forgotten long ago.

And somewhere along the way, the emptiness in the man's heart began to fill with the life he'd found.

"I thought I was saving you," he said one evening, scratching behind Dog's ears. "But maybe it's the other way around."

Moving through the cracks

The darkness lingered,
It was too familiar to name,
its edges pointed, its silence loud.

I moved through it,
not knowing if there was an end
or just more of the same.

Then came the smallest shift—
a glimmer, faint as breath,
moving through the cracks.

It called me forward,
past the truth of what was,
past the walls I built to hold myself in.

The air thickened with the scent of life,
wet earth and wild blooms.

A leaf unfurled,
then another,
until the trees were full,
reaching skyward with hope.

Fear loosened its grip,
its voice fading
beneath the hum of light.
And there I stood,
unshackled,
the sun touched every corner of my skin.

Here, in this open place,
the world offered itself whole—
and for the first time,
I said yes.

XIII

On Time

Fleeting

Time slips between us,
like sand through open fingers
never asking to stay,
only to be held for a breath,
and then gone.

I have seen the stillness in your gaze,
the softness of your touch
when it lingers near,
but never quite meets.

There are spaces between us,
small as a sigh,
where silence speaks louder
than words ever could.

The moments are tender,
like petals barely opened,
and I wonder if you feel it,
the gravity of it,
of something so close yet so far,
so unwilling to wait.

I could reach out,
but my hands remain still,
fingers curled around yours.

In this space, there is only
what we do not say,
what we do not do,
but know.

The light will fade,
and we will not have had enough,
not nearly enough.
But for now,
we are here,
silent in the fleeting glow.

XIV

On Connection

In the quiet of the night

To those who rest alone,
no warmth of hands that hold,
with only shadows for company,
you are not unseen.

The earth cries with your ache,
sings across old villages and towns,
through cities where the lights flicker
in the dark lonely lanes.

There are those who, for a single dusk,
feel the silence fold them in,
and those who carry it,
year after year, like an empty weight.

Yet in the stillness,
you are cradled by an unseen embrace,
for the ache of one
is the ache of many,
and somewhere, under the same moon,
someone else feels the ache, too.

Rest, then,
in the comfort that we all share
this same sorrow,
knowing the night is never truly empty,
and no one is ever truly alone.

"Whoever you are, now I place my hand upon you, that you
be my poem,
I whisper with my lips close to your ear,
I have loved many women and men, but I love none better
than you."
                                                    – Walt Whitman